When the Church

Says 'No'

Helen Thorp

Part-time tutor at Cranmer Hall and
The Wesley Study Centre, Durham
Vocations Advisor, Diocese of Durham

GROVE BOOKS LIMITED
RIDLEY HALL RD CAMBRIDGE CB3 9HU

Contents

In tender memory of
David Smith
1983–2003
A chooser of Life,
undefeated in death.

Acknowledgment

I am indebted to all who over the years have courageously entrusted me with their stories of
rejection and given me the privilege of sharing the depths and yearnings of their journey.

The Cover Illustration is by Jeff Anderson

Copyright © Helen Thorp 2004

First Impression June 2004
ISSN 0144-171X
ISBN 1 85174 565 3

Introduction

1

In the hot, dry summer of 2003 Stephane Jousse, furious at not being accepted as a volunteer fire fighter, deliberately started fires in Provençal forests. Four people died as a result.[1]

Rejection can be dangerous and destructive and it is not just the individual concerned who may be at risk.

In every church there are men and women whose offers of voluntary service have not been accepted. Some may once have been candidates offering for ordained or accredited lay ministry, others will have been voted off church councils or not re-appointed to committees, while yet others will have been passed over in leadership or ministerial involvement.

The church is both the context and the cause of the rejection they suffer. What is expected to be a safe place becomes threatening. Acknowledging and exploring this terrain looks prohibitive to all concerned and there are no maps. While personal and pastoral experience of rejection is common it remains a neglected landscape. There is very little literature available. This is interesting given that the church is founded on one whose calling was to suffer rejection, crucifixion and resurrection.

Whilst personal and pastoral experience of rejection is common it remains a neglected landscape

I will begin by exploring the landscape of rejection. The next and longest chapter argues a theological framework for 'not being chosen.' What Scripture has to say about this is demanding; there are few 'obvious' passages and what is both said and left unsaid challenge our protestations. The temptation is to avoid the task. But this engagement is necessary for the appropriate shaping of our understanding and pastoral approach. Chapter four draws on psychological insights to inform pastoral practice. The later chapters suggest guidelines for the care of those who are not chosen for church office.

Throughout, I write in the belief that the journey through rejection has potential for growth and transformation.

2 Surveying the Landscape:
What Does the Experience of Rejection Look Like?

The experience is unique to each person, but a lot of mature Christians acknowledge that to have an offer of service declined is harder than might have been anticipated.

> I didn't think I cared about being on PCC until I wasn't elected. It was like I had been kicked in the stomach and left gasping and bruised.

A non-recommended ordination candidate talked about 'nothing ever affecting me quite like this' and lamented 'No-one told me what to expect.' Since the church largely operates with volunteers (and there are never enough of them) there is an expectation, particularly with lay ministries, that our offer will be accepted. The pain of rejection is thereby intensified. An applicant for an accredited ministry scheme reflected: 'Because of my experience and background I thought it was a foregone conclusion.' She was 'absolutely devastated' when not accepted. Rejection in the context of Christian service can be so powerful because, in the pattern of Christ, what is offered is the whole self.

> This wasn't like applying for a job; this was 'Here I am—take me!' And they said: 'Thanks but no.'

The rejection is not of a particular set of skills or inappropriate training but of the whole person. Self-esteem is inevitably threatened. 'They've got me wrong!' is the voice that does not recognize self in the perceptions of others. Loss of identity and confidence result: 'I don't know who I am anymore...' said a church officer who had not anticipated stepping down, '...and I don't have the heart to do anything else.' An ordination candidate spoke of '*in limbo* existence' continuing several years after non-recommendation.

Alongside a crisis in self-esteem, faith also can come under threat. Disturbing questions abound:

- Can I ever again trust my discernment of God's voice?
- What kind of God would play games with me like this?
- I do not recognize my God in any of this; where does that leave the church?
- Is there a God or am I just deluding myself?

The experience of rejection can be so threatening to faith and theology that it becomes impossible to make connections between the two. Personal spirituality then begins to lose its authenticity. Some people may leave the church; others lose faith altogether. Images of victimization are common vocabulary.[2] 'After all these years of faithful service they've dumped me out in the cold and left me to die...' said a faithful choir member on being passed over for the Patronal Festival solo. A nominee not chosen for a ministry team described himself as 'robbed' and a woman voted off the Church Council felt herself 'violated.' A number of non-recommended ordination candidates have likened the selection process to emotional and spiritual 'rape.' Such responses can seem rather shocking given that we are talking about the ordering of ministry in the Church of Jesus Christ.

In most contexts there is no intention of inflicting pain, but individuals who have not been chosen often feel themselves misrepresented, misunderstood or unvalued by 'them.' They experience real pain.[3] The powerlessness to redress outcomes or have questions answered compounds the feeling of the selecting body as victimizers.

> What have I ever done that they should treat me like this?

Sometimes the 'victim' is indefinite or vague about the identity of 'them'; in other cases there is a certainty and clarity about exactly who is behind the act of rejection.

With rejection can come the uncomfortable experience of stigmatization. Goffman defines stigma as 'an undesired differentness from what we had anticipated,' and suggests the weight of the burden of stigmatism is related to the levels of acceptance experienced.[4] Thus, both the individual member and the church family are implicated. Where the rejection has occurred within the local Christian body there can be guilt and shame all round:

> When someone else was announced as leader of the ministry team I didn't know where to look or what to say, and neither did anyone else. I was the naked fool and they had taken my clothes.

Where the selection process has been at a regional or national church level the whole local church can feel stigmatized. Supporters of the candidate have expressed frustration that their advocacy has been 'set aside,' their judgment 'put down' and their voice 'left unheard.' Whatever the process, the individual can feel discredited amongst the worshipping body, resulting in either personal withdrawal or distancing behaviour from others, or a combination of both. An awkwardness and embarrassment can intrude into previously easy and supportive relationships leading to isolation and even alienation. One ordination candidate talked of being 'treated like a leper' following non-recommendation, a Reader struggling without a ministry felt 'there was no-one to try to make meaning of this with me' and a woman not elected to the PCC at the third time of offering feared the 'cruel silence and secret ridicule' of those 'friends' who had not given her their vote.

Such experiences of rejection can generate raw emotional responses. Christian communities are generally not at ease with negative feelings and those unable to contain them may be further alienated from fellowship. A minister was bewildered by a lay leader who had been encouraged to retire:

> Where there is conflict he is usually caught up in it somewhere. He never used to be this difficult.

Shock, anger, bitterness, confusion, tearfulness, disillusionment and jealousy are all common to the experience of rejection.

These feelings can continue unresolved for years. They may be repressed and denied, leaving the candidate (and others) surprised by their sudden awkward and explosive expression. Alternatively, feelings may be so near the surface that they spill out uncontrollably and inappropriately in embarrassing outbursts of anger or tears. Absence of feeling is a different consequence, and can last beyond the numbness that is a typical early response to a grief situation. An ordination candidate lost all emotional responsiveness, both positive and negative, for months following a non-recommendation; from his perspective he was 'fine' but his wife increasingly feared she had 'lost' him.

How the affective responses to rejection are acknowledged, expressed and managed affects all significant relationships. Partners and families are vulnerable to unbidden and inappropriate surfacing of displaced negative emotion. A wife complained: 'It's the church that didn't want him, but it's me and the kids who cop it.' Neither anticipating nor being prepared for the changes in the one they know and love, they can be left angry and fearful. Sometimes it is a matter of making temporary allowances until the hurt passes, but where the experience of rejection has been severe the whole relational dynamic may need to be re-negotiated, with the associated stress. My own work with non-recommended ordination candidates suggests that the marriage relationship comes under significant strain, occasionally to breaking point. A failure of pastoral care for the spouse compounds the feelings of hurt, neglect and bitterness towards the church. One husband confessed:

> No one has ever enquired after me in all this. I've missed that. I may never look as if I need care, but if someone would just ask...

The church may not have a duty of care to friends and work colleagues but they, too, may be recipients of displaced emotion, troubled by the consequences of the experienced rejection. It is easier in a secular setting to champion the cause of the individual and dismiss the rejection as outrageous, but this is not always helpful. Some candidates may find themselves in the demanding position of defending the (hurtful) actions of Christians against the critical comments of those outside the church.

An experience of rejection in the body of Christ is never confined to the candidate alone. Others are caught up in the disappointment, confusion and pain. A church sending a member for the testing of a ministry will feel the corporate loss and challenge of a non-recommendation. The congregation can be angered and troubled by the unanticipated outcome, finding the feedback difficult to receive. They may dismiss or discredit the selectors and protest to senior personnel. Those who have encouraged the offering for ministry may feel a weight of responsibility for the suffering inflicted. Caught between regional or national structures and the pastoral needs of the individual and local community the minister/chaplain is in a particularly awkward and delicate position.

Management of the fall-out from an experience of rejection contained within the local church context is even more demanding and divisive because there is no scope to project blame safely beyond the immediate membership. The candidate faces the challenge of continuing in fellowship with those who have done the rejecting, whilst the latter are left with the challenge of taking responsibility for their action and offering appropriate pastoral care. This landscape of rejection is daunting and potentially very threatening, and inevitably the parties involved tend to avoid exploring it. The hard-pressed minister, even if not directly involved in the act of rejection, is usually relieved to collude with the avoidance. Left unaddressed the awkwardness and hurt may fester rather than go away, and in years to come, whenever the fellowship strays inadvertently into that particular landscape, its life can be infected by the bitterness.

How can someone negotiate a way through this experience? Immersion in more acts of Christian service is one way of demonstrating worth. Alternatively, withdrawal from active membership protects against further hurt. The pain of rejection is always unsettling and sooner or later there may be a moving out—out of neighbourhood, employment, local church, denomination or even Christianity. Moving out will not fix the pain of rejection, but some people may need to move out to move on. They may also leave their worshipping community a legacy of guilt and resentment, especially if the ending has not been well-managed.

3

When someone putting themselves forward for church office is recommended for or appointed to that ministry, a partnership of choice is involved.

It is a coming together of divine calling and human discernment. God speaks and his people respond by searching out an understanding of his choice. Whilst the human aspect of the process is usually the presenting problem for those who are not chosen, the underlying issue is the nature of the 'choosing God.' Disturbing questions invite attention. Taking a hard look at Scripture can open up fresh perspectives and insights. Attention is re-focused on theological and spiritual engagement and the challenge of transformation.

The Divine Calling

The Choosing God

The whole canon of Scripture is about the God who chooses. Out of the humanity he has created he chooses a people for himself, and out of his people he chooses individuals for particular purposes and ministry.

The first biblical instance of the selecting God is as early as Genesis 4, the preference for Abel over Cain.[5] It is a passage that has generated both defensive explanation and protest.

> Now Adam knew Eve his wife, and she conceived and bore Cain, saying, 'I have produced a man with the help of the Lord.' And again, she bore his brother Abel. Now Abel was a keeper of sheep, and Cain a worker of the ground. In the course of time Cain brought to the Lord an offering of the fruit of the ground, and Abel also brought of the firstborn of his flock and of their fat portions. And the Lord had regard for Abel and his offering, but for Cain and his offering he had no regard.'(Genesis 4.1–5)

No reason is offered for God's regard for the younger brother and his offering; the experience is factually recorded without comment. There is no indication at this point that Cain has done anything wrong or that God's choice to favour Abel is related to Cain being undeserving. There would seem to be an arbitrariness about it.

Cain, not surprisingly, reacts strongly against God's regard for his brother. Rage and dejection take hold. Significantly, God's response to Cain's negative emotion is neither condemnation nor abandonment. He comes to question and encourage him:

> So Cain was very angry, and his face fell. The Lord said to Cain, 'Why are you angry and why has your face fallen? If you do well, will you not be accepted? And if you do not do well, sin is crouching at the door. Its desire is for you, but you must rule over it.' (Genesis 4.5–7)

Moberly argues that what is translated as 'If you do well will you not be accepted?' is 'almost certainly an inaccurate translation' of the Hebrew. Rather, the literal reading 'Is there not if you do well lifting up?'[6] refers back to Cain's fallen face (vv 5, 6) and carries the meaning of raising his downcast looks. Thus the unhelpful implication that God's preference for Abel is related to Cain's unacceptability is removed. God's words here are not about how to get chosen but about how to live with the not being chosen. He presents Cain with a clear choice: if you work with the lot I have given you—'if you do well'—your disappointment can be transformed (and your face lifted up), but if you do not engage positively with the challenge—'if you do not do well'— you will succumb to the sin which is watching and waiting for you. God recognizes the vulnerability of the disappointed and the struggle that must ensue so as not to fall into sin. His desire is for Cain to find a pathway through the resentment to grace and blessing.

Cain cannot accept the inequity of God's choice or respond obediently to his encouragement. Giving vent to his jealous rage he murders the brother for whom God has regard, bringing on himself the rejection that God's choice of Abel never implied.

> And the Lord said, 'What have you done? The voice of your brother's blood is crying to me from the ground. And now you are cursed from the ground, which has opened its mouth to receive your brother's blood from your hand. When you work the ground it shall no longer yield to you its strength. You shall be a fugitive and a wanderer on the earth.'　　　　　　　　　　　(Genesis 4.10–12)

It could have been otherwise. God's choice of Abel could have worked for Cain's greater good.

The story of two more brothers, Esau and Jacob, is an illuminating commentary on Genesis 4. Again, God would seem to act with a certain arbitrariness in his favouring of Jacob over Esau from before birth. Genesis 25.22, 23 records how Rebekah, sensing the struggle within her womb, enquires of the Lord and is told of God's intention to prefer Jacob over Esau. Romans 9.10–13 picks up the story:

> Though they were not yet born and had done nothing good or bad—
> in order that God's purpose of election might continue, not because
> of works but because of his call—she was told, 'The older will serve
> the younger.' As it is written, 'Jacob I loved but Esau I hated.'[7]

There can be no rationalizing of the inequity of God's choosing. Jacob has done nothing to merit preference and Esau has done nothing to forfeit favour. We are left with mystery. Jacob, not content to trust God's choosing, shockingly robbed Esau of his paternal blessing. Suffering intense grief, 'Esau lifted up his voice and wept' (Genesis 27.38) and the injustice naturally provoked hatred and thoughts of murderous revenge (Genesis 27.41). Isaac's household could no longer safely contain the dangerous emotions and Jacob —and the story of God's chosen instrument—moves away for many years.

In Genesis 33, however, Jacob, returning home, re-encounters his brother and discovers him to be a greater man in both material and spiritual riches. Jacob feared reprisal,

> But Esau ran to meet him and embraced him and fell on his neck and
> kissed him, and they wept.   (Genesis 33.4)

Esau is of the stature of the father in the parable of the prodigal son (Luke 15.20). His eager and forgiving embrace is testimony to a profound spiritual transformation. Unlike Cain, he has 'done well' with the challenge of not being chosen; 'he has mastered the beast of resentment which was waiting to devour him.'[8] Grace was so operative in him that Jacob recognized the divine likeness and character in his brother:

> 'For I have seen your face, which is like seeing the face of God, and
> you have accepted me.'   (Genesis 33.10)

Esau could not change God's choice of Jacob, but he could, and did, co-operate with God to transcend its effects.

As the canon of Scripture unfolds, further examples of God's choosing continue to defy human reason and expectation. Preference would not seem to be on the grounds of moral goodness; most of the heroes of faith in Hebrews 11 have pasts worthy of tabloid exposure. Equally, God's preference did not exclude the devout and spiritually disciplined such as Mary and John the Baptist. Many of God's chosen instruments looked unpromising candidates, without maturity or proven skills; others, like Daniel and Saul of Tarsus were remarkably gifted and impressive.

The grounds for Jesus' choice of apostles are not given. There was a pool of at least 70 disciples and yet the outcome of a night of prayer was the inclusion in the favoured twelve of Judas Iscariot (Luke 6.12–16). Contemporary hopefuls must have suffered bewilderment, jealousy, and pain but their story does not merit a mention in the gospels.[9] God as chooser does not give answers; Rowan Williams talks about 'the inscrutable God' in relation to vocation.[10] Reconciling the mystery and inequity of this God with how we might want him to behave is deeply challenging.

What would seem to be consistently the case, however, is that God's choice of one does not imply unacceptability of another. The love and mercy that was extended to Cain and the grace that worked abundantly in Esau is available to all who wrestle with the challenge of not being chosen.

The Rejecting God

We may not feel comfortable with God as rejecter. He is, however, clearly associated with acts of rejection throughout Scripture. Are there instances of divine rejection in relation to vocation and service?

1 Samuel 15 and 16 invite attention. Saul, the Lord's choice as king (1 Sam 10.14) has been unfaithful in his relationship with God (1 Sam 15.11) and the prophet, Samuel, delivers the hard word:

> And Samuel said to Saul, 'I will not return with you. For you have rejected the word of the Lord and the Lord has rejected you from being king over Israel.' As Samuel turned to go away, Saul seized the skirt of his robe and it tore. And Samuel said to him, 'The Lord has torn the kingdom of Israel from you this day and has given it to a neighbour who is better than you.' (1 Samuel 15.26–28)

The Hebrew word for 'reject' (also translated 'despise' or 'have contempt for') is used most commonly in contexts of spiritual unfaithfulness.[11]

God's rejection of Saul is not arbitrary; it is the direct result of Saul's own rejection of God. As a consequence God withdraws his blessing and earmarks the kingdom for another. Although Saul nominally holds office for some time to come, his kingship is 'dead' from that day. This rejection is quite different from 'not being chosen.' It carries an accusation of spiritual failure and a penalty of divine judgment.

The vocabulary of rejection continues into the next chapter and the process of discerning the neighbour 'who is better than you.'

> The Lord said to Samuel, 'How long will you grieve over Saul, since I have rejected him from being king over Israel? Fill your horn with oil and go, I will send you to Jesse, the Bethlehemite, for I have provided for myself a king among his sons.' (1 Samuel 16.1)

Samuel knows that God's choice is upon one of Jesse's sons—but which one? His gaze is drawn to one (like Saul) with physical presence:

> He looked on Eliab and thought, 'Surely, the Lord's anointed is before me.' But the Lord said to Samuel, 'Do not look on his appearance or on the height of his stature, because I have rejected him. For the Lord does not see as man sees; man looks on the outward appearance, but the Lord looks on the heart.' (1 Samuel 16.6–7)

The verb 'rejected' is the same Hebrew word used of Saul in v 1 (and in 1 Samuel 15.23, 26). The comparison is unavoidable. With Eliab, it is not a matter of God's preference lying elsewhere; rather as God rejected Saul, so he is rejecting Eliab. The implication is that Eliab, through disobedience, has himself rejected God and thereby incurred divine rejection. What the Lord sees in Eliab's heart would seem to be very different from his impressive outward appearance. The text, however, is silent in respect to the nature of Eliab's disobedience and it could equally be argued that, despite the repetition of the verb 'rejected,' here is a case of 'not chosen' rather than 'rejection.' Eliab's angry and contemptuous outburst against David in 1 Samuel 16.28, 29 may indicate a longer standing disobedience and disrespect of God's ways or merely signify a failure to handle disappointment. Scripture does not offer tidy categories.

In relation to Jesse's other sons different language is used:

> Neither has the Lord chosen this one.
> (1 Samuel 16.8, and also vv 9 and 10)

Here the verb 'chosen' (used negatively) is the same Hebrew word that was used of the divine calling of Saul in 1 Samuel 10.24. Eliab was 'rejected' but the other brothers were 'not chosen.' In their case there is no suggestion of divine rejection or judgment.

Where Scripture speaks of God as rejecter we can expect the context to be one of failure to keep covenant promises. Only when his people reject him does God act to reject them.[12] God's rejection of Saul and possibly Eliab are cases in point. Characteristically, however, there is no scriptural use of the vocabulary of rejection in the context of divine calling. God chooses his team. The rest of the players are not rejected; usually they are not mentioned. Whatever the silence may feel like, it does not carry any implication of God as rejecter.

Human Discernment

The story of the experienced and faithful Samuel searching out God's choice of David illustrates the difficulty of human discernment. Samuel must have been shocked that his singling out of Eliab was such a failure of judgment, and bewildered that the parade of Jesse's seven impressive sons did not produce God's chosen one. Of course, no-one had thought of putting forward the little shepherd. Had Samuel not persisted in searching he would have missed David.[13]

In the early church human discernment is characteristically a corporate activity. In choosing a replacement for Judas all the gathered disciples were involved in nominations; after prayer 'they cast lots' to determine which of the candidates God had chosen (Acts 1.23–26). The 'full number of the disciples' is entrusted with the task of choosing deacons (Acts 6.2, 3). In worship and fasting the gathered church at Antioch discern the Spirit's choice of Barnabas and Paul 'for the work to which I have called them' (Acts 13.2). The apostles and elders together with the whole church in Jerusalem chose two of their men to send to Antioch (Acts 15.22). Scripture is silent on the mechanisms used for discernment.

Whilst choosing together under the guidance of the Spirit is the assured practice, discernment is a venture of faith. There would seem to be an absence of divine confirmation; God lets his people get on with the task of appointing church officers. Did they always 'get it right'? We cannot tell. There would have been disappointed candidates at every election and appointment but we do not hear of them. The expectation is an acceptance of outcome and a continuing in committed membership. Guthrie comments:

> Paul has much to say about service which is given out of love without having any official status.[14]

Sometimes, as in Acts 14.23, discernment would appear to rest with just two church leaders. On one occasion, Paul and Barnabas discern differently; Barnabas recommends 'John called Mark' but previous experience of Mark's withdrawal from partnership in mission causes Paul to doubt the choice.

> And there arose a sharp disagreement, so that they separated from each other. Barnabas took Mark with him and sailed away to Cyprus, but Paul chose Silas and departed, having been commended by the brothers to the grace of God. (Acts 15.39, 40)

There is no suggestion that others were included in the discernment; dispute and division ensued. Barnabas stands against the authority of Paul to support Mark, and these verses indicate the isolation of his position. The repercussions would have affected the whole church, and we can imagine the pastoral fall-out.

Later, reservation about Mark changed to strong recommendation:

> Get Mark[15] and bring him with you, for he is very useful to me for ministry. (2 Timothy 4.11)

Was the earlier discernment faulty? Has Mark grown in ministerial stature? Is the issue one of discerning God's time? Any or all of these factors may apply. If we accept Pauline authorship it would seem that even for him discernment could be of a provisional nature, with decisions open to revision. Humanity is vulnerable in its searching out and understanding of God's choice.

Jesus: Chosen for Rejection

When we offer for church office we put ourselves in the way of Christ. His servant ministry discomforted expectations of the Messiah and proved unacceptable to the religious authorities. From his birth outside the inn to his death outside the city there was a resistance to let him in. To be despised, rejected and not held in esteem was the nature of his calling (Isaiah 53.3).

His world did not know him and his own did not receive him (John 1.10, 11). In his last days he suffered abandonment (Matt 26.56), betrayal (Matt 26.48), and denial (Matt 26.69–75). On the cross he cried out to God in total dereliction (Mark 15.34). The chosen one of God was to take on himself the rejection associated with unfaithfulness to the covenant relationship (Isaiah 53.4, 5) and in doing so fulfilled God's purposes (John 12.27). Thus, 'the stone that the builders rejected has become the cornerstone' (Matt 22.42). Here is a calling both cruel and glorious—'Was it not necessary that the Christ should suffer these things and enter into his glory?' (Luke 24.26)—and in embracing it Jesus 'did well.'

What can we learn from Jesus about living fruitfully with rejection?

- *His self-concept and esteem were determined by his relationship with God.* His identity and worth were not dependent upon the values and praise of other people. He had the assurance that his heavenly Father was 'well pleased' with the 'beloved son' (Matt 3.17; 17.5). Confident in God's trust and strong in the knowledge 'that he had come from God and was going back to God' Jesus could humbly strip down to wash feet (John 13.3–5). He knew the stature of his place with God and he needed no other approval or assurance to bolster his own esteem.

- *His framework of belief was large enough to contain the experience of rejection.* He 'set his face to go to Jerusalem' (Mark 9.53) confident that after the suffering would come resurrection (Mark 8.31). Rejection is not the whole story; held within it is the hope of redemption and triumphant life. Jesus took rejection beyond crucifixion; his self-offering enabled God to transform it into fullness of life.

- *In his thinking Jesus kept God's perspective on his experiences of rejection.* In Matt 11.25 he 'thanks' his Father for the divine interventions that caused the scorn he suffered in Matt 11.19. In Luke 10.16 he distinguishes between rejection that is personal and rejection that is directed towards God—and he leaves God to deal with the latter.

- *With regard to his feelings, Jesus did not deny, diminish or hide the emotional pain in the places where rejection really hurt.* He was at ease with his feelings and able to express an emotional response to rejection. The failure of the disciples to keep watch with him in the sorrow of Gethsemane (Matt 26.40) and the abandonment by God that elicited so heart-rending a cry from the cross (Mark 15.34) are obvious examples.

Jesus lived joyously, generously and truthfully. In the whole of his dazzling life he was not chosen once for institutional religious office.

Summary

The Bible does not unfold like a map. It is not easy to read. Narrative material is untidy, incomplete, frustrating, not without silences, and resistant of closure.[16] This is particularly so in relation to calling and discernment. There is no blueprint for the ordering of our corporate life and little or no reference to the needs of those who are not chosen for church office. The searching out of answers to our questions can make for uncomfortable and challenging reflection. But the biblical material does suggest that there is a distinct difference between not being chosen and rejection.

Whilst 'in God's eyes all vocations are of equal value; it is we who perceive them differently'[17] it nevertheless feels a tough calling to not be chosen for a particular office yet still be invited to 'do well' in a life of discipleship. The Servant Son offers ways of living with and beyond rejection that challenge our understanding of identity, theology and faith. Again, we may not like confronting his truth. 'But (if we are wise)' suggests Moberly 'we read Scripture to discover the truth about God and our human situation, which may often mean learning to come to terms with that which initially appears unpalatable.'[18] It is in and through our 'learning to come to terms' that the Spirit graciously works for our transformation.

4 Map Making:
A Psychological Model of the Rejection Experience

Most Christians who offer themselves for a position of service believe that they are 'together people' with the competences and qualities required.

It can be deeply threatening to discover that others seem to have a different perception. An ordination candidate found her sense of identity shaken:

> I thought I had found the right shaped hole for my gifts. The report with its lop-sided review of my vocation left me feeling like a freak.

Carl Rogers, father of person-centred counselling, defines the self-concept as 'an organization of hypotheses for meeting life.'[19] That is to say, how we see ourselves determines how we respond to people and events. Where the self-concept is largely defined by the praise and needs of other people, self-esteem is low. Where it is located more in authentic, personal reality, and thereby more independent of the opinions of others, self-esteem is higher.

For the Christian, esteem is related to how much of our identity is rooted in God. Knowing himself to be the beloved son, Jesus did not need the recognition of the chief priests or the acceptance of the Nazarene synagogue. Other sons and daughters of God can also secure their identity in his love. So Rowan Williams warns against 'inventing' ourselves when our identity comes from standing before the Christ of the gospels.[20] Turning our eyes and hearts from the affirmation of people to trust the affirmation of God is radical discipleship indeed.

Rogers' theory of the self is constructed through personal experience and therefore it is the perception of rejection (however accurate or misunderstood this may be) that matters. What is *heard* may wound more deeply than what was actually said.

When not being chosen for church office constitutes a major loss, the candidate is challenged to review the repertoire of self-images.

> Who am I? What gifting do I have? Can I trust in my abilities? Can I believe the good things church members say about me?

The crisis for the self-concept will inevitably have negative, even dangerous effects:

> If anyone referred to parts of the selectors' report that I could not identify with I felt very threatened. After this 'NO' I just did not have the sense of self-worth that would take any kind of knock.

But Rogers argues that there is an opportunity for restructuring the self which makes for greater integration and freedom of life. Major research on enforced transition by psychologists Adams, Hayes and Hopson finds evidence of the potential for growth in and through rejection.[21]

> One realizes this potential and moves towards it when one fully lets go and fully accepts the situation for what it is, when one dies 'a little death to become larger.' (p 13)

They offer a staged model for understanding the cycle of reactions and feelings that disappointed expectation triggers. There is seldom a neat movement from phase to phase; there will be progressions and regressions unique to each individual. Furthermore, the level of self-esteem at the point of rejection and the importance to the individual of the church office will affect the extent and duration of the resulting stress. Seven stages are identified (in my experience candidates will usually want to short-cut from stage two to stage six) and it is possible to get stuck at any point; skilled intervention may be necessary to enable forward movement. Significantly, esteem is higher at the end of the process than it was at the beginning; this model promises the potential 'to do well' (Gen 4.6–7) in and through demanding challenge.

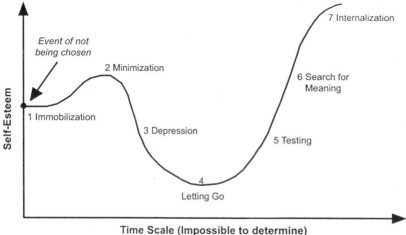

Time Scale (Impossible to determine)

Immobilization is the initial impact of being overwhelmed or frozen up, unable to comprehend. A long-standing church council member recalled the moment when not re-elected: 'I couldn't believe what I was hearing. I just sat there.'

Minimization is characterized by denial, distortion and unrealistic optimism. 'They got me wrong. The whole system is a shambles. I'm better off staying as I am,' sums up many reactions on discovering that an offer for church office has been declined. It is a temporary but important retreat from reality to allow internal forces to re-group and energy to be directed into continuing with life: 'I thought I was fine, that it was all for the best. I convinced myself and everyone else of this,' recalled a non-recommended ordination candidate, 'but I need to admit that I'm far from fine. I feel as though I've stopped, turned in on myself, and no avenue excites me like it used to.'

As the reality of the experience is gradually confronted in the stage of *Depression* there is a fall in self-esteem. The tendency to distort can spin agonizingly out of control, 'They've rubbished my whole life. Everything I do is rubbish,' declared a non-recommended candidate several years after the event. Turbulent emotions, powerlessness, and expressions of blame put stress on relationships (including sexual) and general and spiritual health. 'Most things are without purpose. I go to church in the mindless hope of finding the God I once knew, but perhaps there is no God,' reflected a depressed young man who had made painful sacrifices for his vocational journey. It can be a time of aloneness and dereliction: 'Who else was there who could bear the burden? Nobody seemed to be able to share the pain of rejection. God seemed to have disappeared.'

Underlying these first stages is the continued attachment to what was or might have been. Turning the corner requires an acceptance of the reality for what it is and a decision to actively let go of denied hopes. Stage four, *Letting Go*, demands a significant change in orientation: 'I want to let go of always trying to measure things against what they [the Bishops' Selectors] said. I won't let them destroy me. I want to leave the past behind a bit more.'

Appropriate levels of challenge and support in pastoral care can be crucial at this point, and the above candidate valued the encouragement to take responsibility for her own attitudes and for finding ways of reclaiming herself as a daughter of God; it was not going to be easy.

Clawing back self-esteem through the stage of *Testing*, which is often characterized by energy-generating anger and bursts of activity and experimentation can make for a stormy ride. After a lonely struggle with rejection one man resolved to re-engage with prayer. He visualized the cross and the hands of Jesus 'flung wide in an expansive gesture of welcome' but they became a taunt to him.

In a sudden rage I wanted to hurt the person who had caused my pain. I saw myself picking up a hammer and banging nails into the bleeding hands of the one who hung on there, pinning him to his cross, watching him writhing in agony with each sharp blow.

Suddenly I stopped, shocked at what I saw myself doing. In a flash I was confronted with the stark reality of my emotions.

The Christ who was at ease with his own negative emotions can put us in touch with the pain that we dare not voice, even to ourselves, and offer our authentic selves his acceptance:

I saw that the God who calls me is the God who knows me already better than I know myself. I saw that, despite knowing me God still loves me, and would do anything to heal my pain. I saw that, in fact, he already has.

Testing is also usually accompanied by a tendency to put significant people into categories of ways in which they should or should not have behaved. 'The vicar should listen to what people are saying and be prepared to break rank,' declared someone disappointed to not be included in the pastoral team, and added, 'the team should be visiting more people.'

Gradually there is a shift towards cognitive development, a *Searching* after what all the anger, activity and protest might mean. The individual is more able to stand back, reflect and grow in understanding. This stage can be one of major insight and change, personally, spiritually and theologically. Faith may not be 'the thing I thought it was.'[22] One ordination candidate reflected:

I believed in my vicar's God, a God of all blessing, but I found him to be a cruel and depriving God. I still believe, but my theology has to make room for a dark side of God.

Following the pattern of Jesus, this man was edging towards a framework of belief large enough to contain his experience. Taking the rejection beyond crucifixion was the next challenge. Exploring his discoveries with an experienced spiritual friend who listened deeply, offering both acceptance and different perspectives, was particularly helpful.

The final stage of *Internalization* represents the integration of the experience and the learning that has accompanied it. There is something of the joy, generosity and truth of Jesus in the growth and movement outwards and onwards.

I met someone last week who said: 'You haven't half changed.' And I thought, 'Yeah, I have, I'm so much freer.' I never thought I would say this, but I thank God for my rejection!

5

Preparing for the Journey

Early Identification of the Pastoral Issues

Who are the people most vulnerable to an experience of rejection? Recognizing those who have the potential to be deeply pained can alert us to appropriate levels of pastoral care. Jesus had particular concern for those with needs that others simply missed. Here are some things to look out for:

Low Self-Esteem

When self-worth is largely determined by the praise and needs of others there is little inner confidence to withstand setback. The person who has 'lived for the church,' whose membership has been shaped by 'what the church expects of me,' is especially at risk.

A History of Loss or Disappointed Expectation

Unrealized hopes of ministry can disturb and compound earlier experiences. Childhood losses compounded by recent unresolved bereavement or setback are a particularly potent mix.

An Image of God and a Theology that Cannot Accommodate the Challenge of the Experience

Either the bleakness of the rejection or the inscrutable nature of God has to be denied, with the accompanying loss of personal or spiritual authenticity and loss of reality.

Definite and High Expectations of the Christian Life and the Ordering of the Church's Ministry

Where trust is implicit and has never been challenged or disappointed, discovering the church and its personnel can bear a marred image of God may be deeply threatening to faith and membership.

Heavy Investment in the Ministry Role for Which the Person has Offered

Those who have always wanted a particular church office and followed the calling with persistence and at great cost have difficulty accepting that they may not be chosen.

Poor Support Systems

Lonely, damaged and misunderstood church members who do not naturally belong to any network may need sensitive care.

Experience of Abuse (Sexual, Physical, Emotional)

This is usually a hidden factor but one to be alert to. Abuse and rejection are strongly linked by the experience of powerlessness. Candidates with a history of abuse are surprised how rapidly a rejection in church life can disturb painful memories and feelings, although it may take a while for them to see the connection.

The experience of rejection is less destructive and more creative where it is understood from the beginning as one possible outcome of the choosing process. Rejection did not come as a nasty shock to Jesus; he was prepared for the cost of his journey of obedience.

How can we prepare for the possibility that an offer of ministry is just that—an offer that may or may not be accepted? Here are some suggestions for good pastoral practice:

- *Be courageously clear about the nature and duration of the office, the process of selection and the potential cost of outcomes.* Check that the risk of not being chosen is understood.

- *Think about the use of language.* Our choice of vocabulary can reinforce feelings of rejection. Do the words we use reflect accurately the nature of the event? Phrases like 'not get through' (or in, or on) and 'turned down' are associated with contexts of failure and inadequacy. Can we find different words and images to better describe what is going on when someone is not chosen for church office? One disappointed candidate put it this way, 'I got on the plane for Italy but it landed in Poland.'

- *Encourage an engagement with relevant biblical material.* Explore the difference between rejection and not being chosen, and what it might mean 'to do well.'

- *Never make assumptions about the outcome.* Comments such as 'You'll get elected' and 'You'll be fine' can impose a heavy burden of expectation. Challenge the culture of assumption with the question, 'How do you know?'

- *'Speak the truth in love' to discourage the investment of energy in pursuing a church office for which the necessary gifts or personal and spiritual maturity is lacking.* Delaying or avoiding the hard word only makes for more hurt later.

- *Take responsibility for your role in the discernment process.* There will always be a duty of prayer and honest feedback. Integrity in writing references, holding to appropriate boundaries of confidentiality and guiding the responses of others may also require attention. Where the outcome is unwelcome the delivery of a professional and accountable process becomes hugely important; attention to detail in any feedback or report is essential.

- *Explore the possibility of rejection at an early stage* and encourage shared exploration with other significant people caught up in the process.[23]

- *Discuss how outcomes will be communicated.* Where it is possible, ask the candidate to choose how, when and with whom the information is shared. Respect the agreed procedure.

- *Encourage conversation exploring what might be appropriate pastoral support.* Do not assume you know what will be most helpful. Listen carefully and remember the candidate's preferences. 'I did not want sympathy,' said an applicant not chosen for an accredited lay ministry. 'Sympathy has never helped me.'

Accompanied Journey: Suggestions For Pastoral Support

6

What Makes For Effective Accompaniment?

There is no 'ministry pack' for accompanying those who have not been chosen for church office. In my own work over the years, however, I have come to see the importance of the following.

Clarity about the Role and Support of the Carer
- Sorting out the various roles I have in relation to this person. I may be their minister, spiritual director, friend, counsellor, employer, and more. Any or all of these roles may be caught up as I share this journey. Are they all appropriate? Which are the more difficult roles to carry? Helping someone withdraw from a local church context and move to another place of worship, for example, can be demanding if their contribution was significant and I am the minister being left behind! How will I manage this tension?

- I may have served a very particular role in relation to the person's offer for ministry. In the Anglican Church the Diocesan Director of Ordinands, who prepares the candidate and the sponsoring papers for a Bishops' Conference, is a case in point. What are my responsibilities following a non-recommendation outcome? Where am I uncomfortable or uncertain? How and with whom can care be appropriately shared?

- Can I recognize the boundaries of my responsibility and competence? Am I able to refer on to other more appropriate personnel and specialists?

- How is my personal support network? Where can I turn for wise counsel? To whom can I entrust my concerns?

The Quality of the Caring Relationship
- Laying aside my own assessment so that I might hear what the candidate, God, and any report may be saying. How hard this can be!

- Treasuring both the worth of what has been offered and the call to offer it.

- Accurately assessing the spiritual maturity and emotional intelligence of the candidate and working appropriately and respectfully. Some people are capable of and ready for demanding change; others are not.

- Faithful, attentive listening, with supportive feedback and gentle challenge.

- Staying with the pain, and resisting the temptation to find escape routes or short cuts out of difficult emotional landscapes.

- Holding on to my own integrity and not colluding with the distortion or denial of reality. Offering different perspectives can be the catalyst to move the process on.

- Affirming the candidate's giftedness and intrinsic worth, and offering specific evidence for my comments.

- Acknowledging my own learning and enrichment from the shared journey.

Informed Pastoral Practice

- Not being fooled by the 'minimization stage'; assurances of well-being are no guarantee of lasting recovery. Unthreatening, continued contact gives a clear message of care; the occasional phone call, card or gentle inquiry over time is always appreciated.

- Being aware of the common expectation of candidates to move from minimization to meaning-making without engaging with the in-between stages of Adams' model (the result is often more failure and discouragement). Offering a framework for understanding transition and what is involved in achieving it can enable significant self-acceptance and movement.

- Watching for signs of readiness to address unresolved issues and making myself available as and when needed.

- Resisting suggesting other roles and tasks until the rejection has begun to be explored meaningfully. Patient waiting on God is always rewarded.

- Being alert to the pastoral needs of partners and other significant people, and seeking to make appropriate provision to support them.

- Remembering that some people need to move out to move on, how can I enable the making of good endings and considered new beginnings?

Some Tools for the Task

To Assess Progress

- Looking at the Adams graph and mapping current position.
- Identifying the 'sticking' places.
- Asking what needs to happen to enable forward movement.

To Help Engage with the Pain of the Experience

- Invite the candidate to write a letter (which will not be sent) to those responsible for the selection outcome telling them the impact of their action. Encourage spontaneous, uncensored responses, the words coming out as angrily, brutally and shockingly as they want.

  What might then be done with this letter? Could it be a tool for prayer? How might it be kept or disposed of?

  Then you could ask the candidate to stand in the shoes of the recipients and respond to the first letter. Suggest that the recipients may have received and understood the immensity of what they have done, or maybe not. Invite the candidate to work instinctively. What might be done with this letter?

- Could the candidate write the experience in narrative form? This can be done in the first person from different perspectives—through the candidate's own eyes, then through the eyes of other significant people or parties.

- How about drawing the pain? What does it look like? What images and colours best express the experience?

Ways in Through Theology

Some questions for the candidate to explore:

- How was God understood before the experience of rejection? How is God understood now?
- What Scriptures authentically reflect your experience?
- What are difficult passages or promises of Scripture for you now?
- What aspects of your belief have been challenged or changed through your experience of rejection?
- What have you learned about 'the choosing God'?

Ways in Through Prayer

Some exercises to suggest to the candidate:

- What passages or verses of Scripture are speaking to you at the moment? Spend time reflecting on how they are addressing your pain and what perspectives they are bringing into your experience.

- Meditate on the Christ who was chosen for rejection, who was never allowed into the church of his day and who suffered in public desolation on the cross. What images of the crucifixion resonate with you? Where does your story fit into the greater canvas of his story? Can you find some meaning in the mystery of redemptive suffering?

- Draw or picture for yourself the details on the canvas of your vocation. Ask Jesus to help you clearly discern what are the core details of his calling on your life. Seek his redemption and restoration of the damage inflicted by the rejection experience. Ask him to show you clearly the details you are being asked to relinquish, and to give you grace to mourn their loss and let them be taken away. Invite him to stay in the picture with you—even when you are not acknowledging or wanting his presence. Ask forgiveness for the times you have pushed him out of the frame.

- Look out for images and symbols of your pain and outrage that both capture and articulate something of your experience and perhaps bring a different perspective to your suffering. Spend time with these, maybe in the fellowship of others who have known the rawness of undeserved pain.

- Seek the wisdom of Christ in discerning when you have sufficiently explored and understood your pain so as to be ready to ask for the grace to open yourself up to his forgiveness flowing into and through you. It is not natural to forgive the pain of rejection, and you may also need to ask Jesus to give you patience with yourself in this crucial task. Forgiving others will release them from the bonds of anger with which you hold them—and which in turn constrain you. Only forgiveness cuts through the power that you have over each other; for the victimized, withholding forgiveness is an exercise in keeping power. (Something you may want to think about!)

Liturgical Resources

These may involve creative adaptation of existing material or the writing of new material, perhaps in conjunction with the candidate. It may, after consultation, seem appropriate to include others in this ministry.

- Confession and the receiving of absolution can be significant in enabling forward movement.

- Prayer for healing of emotional pain and spiritual wounds may be especially relevant in the stages of depression and letting go.

- Some liturgical recognition of the end of transition-making can release a candidate into God's future.

The Challenge of the Journey

In a sermon on vocation the Archbishop of Canterbury delights in a God who chooses us, 'weak, sinful and silly as we are' for 'the privilege of loving and serving him.' He then adds, 'at least for those of us who are chosen. There is a bit of a problem with the rest.'[24]

How refreshingly honest to acknowledge, rather than deny or ignore, that when it comes to not being chosen for church office 'there is a bit of a problem'!

It is a problem not just for disappointed candidates. It invites the loving and rigorous attention of the whole church. It challenges us to revisit our biblical theology, re-examine our spirituality, reshape our pastoral care and review our language of discernment. What an opportunity to open ourselves to new depths and discoveries of life in the Spirit!

But because we are working in a 'problem' landscape there are no quick and easy solutions. This is particularly tough for those ministering at the sharp and bruising end of pastoral care and for those who are receiving (or not receiving) it. There is the potential to 'get it wrong' (again) and the temptation to give up persevering ('we're getting nowhere').

Because we are working in a 'problem' landscape there are no quick and easy solutions

Then, unexpectedly, even in the darkness and confinement, a heavy stone begins to move and we know the grace of resurrection power. And however long it takes (and it may be a very long time) this can be a journey into new life.

My prayer for this booklet is that it will encourage and begin to equip more men and women to risk venturing into the 'problem' landscape. Can we humbly attend the journey of those who, like Cain, are called 'to do well' by moving through rejection into the future of God's choosing? They need our care; we need to learn from their stories.

Notes

1   Pierre Thebault Draguignon, Reuters, 30 July 2003.
2   Such images tend to be used descriptively rather than diagnostically.
3   Lieberman's experiments involving the scanning of the brain's pain centre have shown that 'a response to social exclusion is remarkably similar to what is seen as a response to physical pain.' Reported in *The Guardian*, 10 October 2003.
4   Goffman, *Stigma: Notes on the Management of a Spoiled Identity* (London: Penguin, 1968).
5   I am indebted to Walter Moberly and his paper, 'Is Monotheism Bad for You?' forthcoming in R P Gordon (ed), *The God of Israel* (CUP, 2005) for insights into the stories of Cain and Abel and Jacob and Esau.
6   In its catalogue of exemplars of faith Hebrews 11.4 , making a different point, refers to Abel's 'more acceptable sacrifice.' Lane (Word Biblical Commentary, *Hebrews 9–14*, 1991) comments that 'the lack of detail in Genesis 4 invited elaboration in the subsequent Jewish tradition' (p 333). Biblical writers and scholars are fascinated by the mystery of God's favouring of Abel.
7   The Hebrew idiom means 'I preferred Jacob to Esau.'
8   Walter Moberly, 'Is Monotheism Bad for You?'
9   As with others who are 'not chosen' in Luke 10.1, Acts 6.3–6, 15.2, 22.
10   Rowan Williams, *Open to Judgment* (London: Darton, Longman and Todd, 1994) p 172.
11   Compare Hosea 4.6—the priests who have rejected knowledge of God and truth will in turn be rejected by God. Note, however, God does not reject a blameless man in Job 8.20.
12   The early chapters of Jeremiah offer many examples.
13   Interestingly, there is no suggestion in the text that David had a personal calling (compare Jeremiah 1.4–10). God's choice of David is dependent upon Samuel's discernment.
14   D Guthrie, *New Testament Theology* (Leicester: IVP, 1981) p 760.
15   Mark was a common name. However, Col 4.10–14, Phil 24, and 2 Tim 4.11 all refer to the same group of names, which include Mark, the cousin of Barnabas, by implication identifying that Mark with the Mark of Acts15.39.
16   Richard Bauckham, *Bible and Mission: Christian Witness in a Post-Modern World* (Grand Rapids, MI: Baker Academic, 2003) pp 92, 3.
17   John Adair, *How to Find your Vocation* (Norwich: Canterbury Press, 2000) p 40.
18   Walter Moberly, *Can Balaam's Ass Speak Today?* (Grove Biblical booklet B10) p 23.
19   Carl Rogers, *Client Centred Therapy* (London: Constable, 1951) p 501.
20   *Open to Judgment*, p 205.
21   J Adams, J Hayes, B Hopson, *Transition: Understanding and Managing Personal Change* (London: Martin Robinson, 1976).
22   C S Lewis, *A Grief Observed* (London: Faber and Faber, 1961) p 36. Lewis speaks of the impact of suffering on his own faith as the knocking down of a house of cards, which has to be rebuilt and rebuilt.
23   A list of questions particularly relevant to the preparation of candidates offering for ordained ministry can be found in my chapter in Gordon Kuhrt, *Ministry Issues* (Church House Publishing, 2001) p 117.
24   Rowan Williams, *Open to Judgment*, pp 172–3.